Stand On the Mic Stand

Stand On the Mic Stand

LOVE YOURSELF WORSHIPPER, YOU ARE GOD'S SINGER OF SONGS

Tarupiwa Muzah

RWG Publishing

CONTENTS

RWG Publishing
PO Box 596
Litchfield, IL 62056
https://rwgpublishing.com/
Published in the United States of America

1

~

Prefer Yourself

Bible verse: Mathew 22 verse 39
Love your neighbor as you love yourself.

Oh, not me, Oh Lord, how can I stand on the mic stand.

All I know is to pretend like it's not in me, or I'm not the one. Better people are there to do it. But look now, the way I avoid the mic is the same way I avoid the people. It seems like I'm full of hate, but no. Now, I see, I don't love myself enough. Others seem to jump at the opportunity and put their foot in front like they are talented more than me.

I don't want to compete, but now, I envy those who love the competition. They seem to have something I don't have: They prefer themselves. They call themselves number 1, even when they seem like wanting. I seem too shy, but the overly shy attitude I heard its self-hate. Now, I have to change, Oh Lord, I need your help.

I have plenty of reasons to love myself. He said - Do not fret; the anointing is for the benefit of all. He called me anointed. He compared me to Joseph. He said, look at him; he benefited many. He even said this other day- You are the man, remember, he said- stand, a boy is a man & a man is a boy. He even said -You are great; the wisdom inside of you is going to help many. So, why not prefer myself? I was given that voice. He appeared in my closed room when I was worshipping alone. I even declare and sing about all these many times in my walks. But the moment I reach the church, another voice seems to ring a louder bell. The voice of the scars that I have, the failures, the disappointments, the shame, and the goals unfulfilled.

So, to prefer myself isn't that easy, I pass the chance, that's my usual stance. Oh, what's so great about the mic and the stand anyway. I want to play the background – that's humility. I thought it was until I read one day, the book by Stormie. She was told that she is proud not to stand and sing. Proud, yes, because it means she didn't want to be vulnerable. Stand in front, make the mistakes, all in his name, and all for his glory. She had to get away from such an attitude and do it. She said, OH Lord, I'm not a singer, the Lord said-You are, the one I give my song is my singer.

God has given me his song, so I have to prefer myself- Jesus You Are Faithful King- that worship song I heard in a dream. So, it's pride not to stand on the mic stand. It seems like I want to avoid the comments and mistakes.

Sometimes, we look down when he wants us to look up. Sometimes, we refrain when he wants us to embrace the chance. We have to say, me, me. I can do that. Lead and stand on the mic stand. Yes, he wants us to love others; he has a formula for us to do that. He says as you love yourself. He equips us, gave us gifts, skills, abilities, and all that. All this for us to be like David and say, me I can go & kill that Goliath. David preferred himself. We have to; we are anointed, meaning God with us. When we prefer ourselves, we trust that he won't let us down. He will use us for his glory.

Let's pray & say

Oh Father, help me to prefer myself, to love myself so that I can love others. Give me the grace to grab the opportunity, to sing for your glory, I worship you today, in Jesus' name. Amen.

2

BRAG

Bible verse: 1 Corinthians 1 verse 31
So that, as it is written, Let the one who boasts, boast in the Lord.

You are right. I'm not feeling myself. Alright, I know God chooses the weak things of this world. But people have a way of showing you your weak spots. How can you brag at that moment? How can I stand on the mic stand, I feel down and out, I don't measure up to the measure they measure me with. I tend to be fast to agree. They say you are weak, I say yes, they say you are shy, I say yes. They say you are unqualified, I agree.

David was nothing also, coming from tending the few sheep. They reminded him of the facts. Yes, the facts were true, but something else was bigger than the facts. He was a chosen vessel; he was anointed, and the Holy Spirit was through him. He had experiences of victory. So, what did he do, brag about that, oh yes, for sure?

Can't I do the same, weak as I am? Only I have to remember how I was called by Mrs. Rose – the employer at the time. I was in my room singing the song called-For whom thou oh Lord has blessed is blessed forever. I was thanking my God, and it led to an instant breakthrough.

So, my singing is approved, I see. It has God' s seal of the Holy Spirit on it. Yes, I can brag about that. I know for sure that standing on the mic stand is meant for me: the one who has won the battle before through God's grace.

Yes, I was so used to complain about the facts, but since God's power came, I forget the facts & brag about his presence. You have to brag about the Lord; what he did through you, he can do it again. Goliath spoke the facts, and he said- look, you are just a kid, you come at me with sticks. You have no experience, but that didn't stop David; he didn't listen to the voice of facts. He said, it's the Lord I brag about, it's the Lord who will fight for me. I come in his name, and he won the battle.

Sometimes, we take shame when he wants us to take pride in him. Occasionally, we keep silent when he wants us to speak out. All that he made us see he wants us to brag about it so that we can be strong to act and not feel intimidated by facts, situations, and opinions of others.

The other time I woke up in the morning and discovered that I couldn't swallow any food. I had pain in my stomach, so I decided to take a walk. I then started to sing a song, saying a verse – His divine power has granted all things to us. My healing belongs to me. So, when I came back, to my surprise, the pain had gone, I could eat now with not even any sign of irritation. Glory to God.

The other time I was walking in the streets and singing. A lorry came from another direction and was about to hit me. It hit another car and was coming towards me, but I escaped because an angel of the Lord protected me. All this came through singing in his presence.

Pray & say

Oh, Holy Father, you are with me. You gave me experiences of your glory, help me to boast in you so that, in turn, I will sing for your glory as I trust you to do it again. I worship you today, thank you in Jesus Christ' s name. Amen.

3

Prepare Yourself

Bible verse: Proverbs 24 verse 27

Prepare your work outside, get everything ready for yourself in the field & after that, build your house.

Oh, help me, God, I can't go with these. I'm not used to them. Why do you want me to talk, or do a presentation to people? Oh, people, you want me to Pastor. You want me to preach and do what others do. Be like the ones who are called of God – the ministry material.

Saul thought every warrior takes the Armor, and that was his view of the battle gear. He had seen it happen all the time, Oh Lord, I'm too weak for that.

Long back in high school, I remember myself running from an impromptu speech contest. Oh, I hate talk, that never was in me, never my brand. That's a weight people wants me to carry because I said I'm a ministry type. David said he was a warrior. He can fight that giant. But look at what people do, they give him what he didn't prepare with. Oh, thank you, God, because I see that you don't work that way. You are so faithful. When you command something, it's deposited already in that person. You don't make a demand for something that is not there. You don't create a failure, and you create a winner. What you don't prepare with, you don't win with.

Oh, help me, God, because I have to love myself. I have to see that I already took the chance to prepare myself. The thoughts of people are not God' s thoughts. He says, stand on the mic stand, not for talk, please people, bear with me. But to use the weapon that I prepared myself, which is good ministry. To stand on the mic stand to worship, to sing is best for me. Its a disregarded weapon, it's like a sling and five smooth stones, but look, it wins the war. Worship and song, can it be that important? In war, in battle, God says Yes.

If it's singing, my hesitation is not that fast, because I'm used to it. I have been singing since I was a toddler. I remember that we composed and used to perform at four years of age. The song was called "Jobho Mapisarema," meaning Job & Psalms. I have been singing ever since that time.

So, when God says, Stand on the mic stand, it means I'm ready, he's been watching me getting prepared. He has been preparing me. To love yourself is to say no, no to doing what's not prepared in you. You will look like a fool. Stop being tricked by people. To love yourself is to focus on what you are so used to. You are already an expert in that. You are ready to battle. Excellence comes with time. You did prepare yourself, but the direction is not common.

People think every minister is a preacher, a speaker, a teacher. Look at yourself; you were singing, singing, and singing. Stand on the mic stand, do what you do so easily, that's what you have been called to do. Victory does not come through the weight of an Armor. Who said it should be that complicated. Worship, worship, and worship, let those who preach do what they do. You don't compete with people, but with what God put inside of you.

What you call a habit is your calling, it's being commanded now, it must come out of you. Go with a sling and a stone. When people trouble you to pick a wrong lane, say No, refuse. Say oh yes, I will stand on the mic stand, but to sing and worship because I'm prepared enough to do that, and not this other thing.

Sometimes, you do what's hard for you when he wants you to do what's easy. Sometimes, you say yes when he wants you to say no.

Pray & say

Oh, Father, no chance escapes me. I bear the fruit, and you prepare me, thank you, Father. You got me ready to sing for your glory; you gave me the passion and made me so used to it. Now, help me to focus & not be distracted. Thank you for your grace in Jesus' name. Amen.

4

APPEAR

Bible verse: John 7 verse 4

For no one works in secret if he seeks to be known openly if you do these things show yourself to the world.

Oh Lord, how can I appear? I'm afraid of what people might say. Okay, what if I'm so good at it, I'm afraid because they might envy me, they might try to stop or hinder me. It's a risky venture. Look, see, many run from it. How many people want to stand on the mic stand, a few, why? It's not because the rest have no ability, but its the fear factor. People might laugh at me; people will be jealous of me and hate me. So, most times, I prefer to be not there, and yes, for sure that way, no one will say anything.

I'm afraid of becoming the talk of the town. Appearance is where you appear, energy used, but more courage is needed. You will never volunteer to minister if you are afraid of threats. David appeared when all others were running away from Goliath. The giant was a threat to life itself. You can die, you can cry, let's run and not even try. How many are resisting to follow the will of God because of being afraid of persecution? But by much tribulations, we enter the Kingdom of God, the bible says.

You will never do anything of significance if you are paralyzed by fear. You must fear the fear itself. My Spiritual Father, Prof Ezekiel Guti – before he met a preacher, he met God. Before he began the ministry: Zaoga Forward in Faith international, he was seeking God in the bush one day, and something happened. He heard thick music from the Heavens, and a voice said- Fear not, sin not. Through that revelation, the ministry has grown and now reached more than 140 nations. He has been preaching for more than 70 years non-stop. Only that word of no fear has made him victorious. For sure, fear hinders ministry. Yes, he was threatened many times, persecuted many times, faced near-death experiences many times. Jealous people tried to hinder him many times, but he stood with the word of fear not.

How can I have this courage and no fear? Oh, the answer is Sin not. The righteous are as bold as a Lion, but the evil flees when no one pursues, the bible says. So, as you sin not, you will fear not. Look at Jesus, our Lord, and savior. He was not afraid of the cross. He despised the shame, he was holy, and he died and rose again on the third day, By his blood, we are now free from all our transgressions. He did ministry proficiently without hindrance.

Oh Lord, I don't want to be afraid of people' s faces. You say, stand on the mic stand, and I want to do it without fear. I want to worship you without fear, to express my gratitude in songs, even when persecuted — boldly confessing your goodness and mercy. You have to appear on the battle line; God will be with you and take over. He will give you the strength to overcome. Yes, it's a risky venture. You will lose friends, and you will have enemies, you will have fake friends who are plotting your downfall. But in all this, you are more than a conqueror.

To love yourself is to be bold and clean, be courageous, and win.

David was bold, and he appeared before the battle line when others were fleeing. No, God has not given us the Spirit of fear. No, the Spirit makes you love yourself, be bold, have a sound mind, and have self-control.

Sometimes, we hide when he wants us to appear. Sometimes, we shrink, when he wants us to stretch, we run away, when he wants us to be available and be there.

Yes, they talk because you sing, you worship. Yes, they comment because you are on the move. Don't be afraid to be a star; don't hide the light. Let your light so shine before men, that they may see your good works and give glory to your Father. You can't light a lamp and put it under a bushel, no, you light a lamp to put it on a stand. A city on a hill cannot be hidden. Don't hide, don't be afraid of what they say and what they do to you. You are God's Masterpiece created to do good works that he prepared beforehand for you to do. Love yourself and be who you are. A worshipper. God's chosen one – God's singer of songs.

They were threatening Joseph, saying divorce your wife, Mary, but he refused. This is because what was conceived in her was of the Holy Spirit. Joseph saw that he had to take her; he had to follow what God said. Be bold like Joseph. Never mind people's views or their envious behavior. Never mind enemies, be strong. Express that excellence without fear. God is your rewarder and protector. Not even a hair of your head can fall without him commissioning it. He has the final say.

Pray & say

Oh, Father, thank you for the boldness to stand and minister. Thank you for the Holy Spirit that gives me the courage, help me, and strengthen me, oh Lord, as I worship you. Thank you for your love. Perfect love casts out all fear. I'm not afraid because I trust in your unfailing love for me, thank you, Father, in Jesus Christ's name. Amen.

5

Release It

Bible verse: 1 Corinthians 15 verse 10

But by the grace of God, I am what I am, and his grace toward me was not in vain. On the contrary, I worked harder than any of them though it was not I, but the grace of God that is with me.

Oh Lord, I don't want to do a work that I'm not graced to do. I don't want to do an action that has no flow of oil in it. I don't want to sing if it's not you Holy Spirit singing through me. That would be a dry song, that would be an effort of the flesh. There is no rest in such a type of effort. There is no joy. That action has no flow to it, it's so hard, and no victory comes from it.

The blessing of the Lord makes rich and adds no toil. There is no toil to an action that is so full of blessings. Stand on the mic stand, oh yes, now I can stand because you called me. Before you told me, before you commanded it, I could not act. I could not do it because I hesitated to do a work that has no blessing. Your command, Oh, Lord, is your blessing. Things flow when grace is part of the equation.

How many things are people forcing themselves to do when they are not graced to do it? When you see something becoming more of toil, leave it, refuse it – it's flesh, not Spirit. Oh, sweet Holy Spirit, when you ordain a prayer, it's effortless and yields incredible results. It's like it's you who is praying it. It's so perfect; it is heard and answered. It is a prayer constructed to his glory.

Look at David, that action was not natural; it was not toiling; it was straight to the target. He was graced to do it. He didn't even do it; the grace made that release of the smooth stone straight to the forehead of Goliath. He was led; he was not in action. Oh, Lord, I don't want to be in the singing, I don't want to be in the worshipping. I also don't want to be in this writing. Let grace be the singer; things happen nicely; the anointing flows smoothly and hits the target. He wins the battle, the Lord, he is a mighty warrior. Yes, problems are there, but things flow until you win.

This other day I dreamt of a title of a book called-The Day I Raised My Hands, a worship devotional. I saw that little book in a dream—everything, from the cover, the back cover, and the title. Then I woke up. I knew that I was not going to write that little book. The grace was going to write it for me. The action is going to flow because God's blessing is part of it. Yes, through grace, it was written. Now, I have written many books, but the worship devotional is the only one I saw in a dream. In the dream, I also heard someone say - its creativity, oh yes, for sure, it got published, and now it's impacting many.

I love God's instruction; it is God's grace. It's his blessing to release what you have. Don't fake to have it, and it will become a toiling work. God will not be part of it. Many have started their endeavors only through emotions. Many have started businesses only through pressure or ambition or copying someone. You say I want to have this, or I wish to be this. You need the grace to release the gift, and you need the grace to act and hit the target.

You don't need to do anything in your strength; you will not be effective. That worship song that I talked about earlier called – Jesus You Are Faithful King. I dreamt of that song. I heard it in a dream. In the dream, I was told to look at this other Elder. He was wearing a white suit. The song was being sung by a long-time friend of mine named Blessing. Then I woke up and something unusual happened later after some months. That Elder I saw in the dream came to our local church and said he wants to see me after church. I then saw him, and he introduced me to a Lady from the UK.

That Lady, after some time, send me money. As I went to collect the money, I found out that there was a studio at that place of collection – at number 7 Belgravia. Then later again, she sends me another amount. Now, this time, the money was enough, and we recorded that song in that studio. So, as you can see, the dream gave me a worship song, the sponsor of that song, and even the studio to record that song. Isn't that amazing?

We released it; grace made it all happen smoothly. For sure, we didn't do it. It was all done for us. It was a blessed endeavor. Who knew that a stone could sink in the forehead of a Giant unless power and grace were part of that release, the act would not have been supernatural. When God speaks something or commands something, know that it has already happened. So, all you have to do is to release it, let him do it through you. Let him stand on the mic stand through you.

There is grace released already on that stand, sing, worship, do it without toiling – It's a blessed endeavor.

Sometimes, we rush, when he wants us to wait for his blessing, his grace, and his instruction. Sometimes, we hesitate when he wants us to act on what he told us we are. What he showed us, let us proceed and release it for his glory. Yes, for sure, we have the victory. David took the head of Goliath, and he had the victory. He was graced to do it, and it was done.

Pray & say

Oh, Holy Father, thank you for your grace and blessing. You are not a man that you should lie, you said it, and you made it happen. You said let there be light, and light came. So, I worship you; I do it through your Spirit. Thank you as I act by faith expecting victory, I receive it as I release it in Jesus's name, Amen.